EVER
SINCE
I
DID
NOT
DIE

THE ARAB LIST

Ramy
Al-Asheq

EVER
SINCE
I
DID
NOT
DIE

Translated by
Isis Nusair

Edited by
Levi Thompson

LONDON NEW YORK CALCUTTA

SERIES EDITOR: Hosam Aboul-Ela

Seagull Books, 2024

Preface and Original Texts
© Ramy Al-Asheq, 2021

Originally published in Arabic by
Bait Elmouwaten Publishing House, Beirut–Damascus, 2016

First published in English translation by Seagull Books, 2021

Introduction and English Translation © Isis Nusair, 2021
Afterword © Levi Thompson, 2021

ISBN 978 1 8030 9 454 0

British Cataloguing-in-Publication Data
A catalogue record for this book is available
from the British Library

Typeset by Seagull Books, Calcutta, India
Printed and bound by WordsWorth India, New Delhi, India

Contents

Translator's Introduction

This collection was written between 2014 and 2016, and published in Arabic in 2016 as part of a series titled *Syrian Testimonies*. Depicting Ramy Al-Asheq's journey in the aftermath of the Syrian Revolution in 2011, these are texts from his different locations and multiple displacements in Syria, Jordan and Germany. Though he wonders about the meaning of poetry and what makes or hurts poetry, Al-Asheq refuses to classify this collection. In a 2017 interview, he described poetry as an end in of itself rather than a means to an end,[1] and added that his texts go beyond him as an author to build their own world. Speaking about the impact of the war and how massive the loss was—loss of houses, homelands, memories, families, even one's self—he wondered whether they actually survived, and how writing was all that he had left.

Refusing binaries and urging us to think about continuums of violence and displacement, Al-Asheq challenges our conceptions of masculinity and heroism and presents transformative forms of being created through and despite the war. In this depiction, he intersects the private with the public, the personal with the political. As he traverses multiple locations and psyches, he shares what he encounters along the way. The form and content of what is shared may be all that remains.

---

1 Isis Nusair, 'Interview with Ramy Al-Asheq' (13 April 2017). Available at: https://www.jadaliyya.com

Al-Asheq traces the effects of war and militarization without sensationalization or objectification, and declares his hate of totalitarian, patriarchal countries. His rejection of boundaries and state lines is reflected in the stereo-types he breaks, especially when writing about refugees. Al-Asheq simultaneously recalls memory and longing as he renounces homelands. Yet, he refuses to cling to death. He also refuses any form of othering as illustrated in 'The Refugee and the Other, the Other Refugee'. He is constantly crossing borders and rejecting all forms of estab-lished conformity.

Al-Asheq associates the homeland and freedom with women's bodies, a conventional representation in relation to the body of the nation which is simultaneously main-tained and challenged throughout the book. Women's bodies become a site for contesting power structures and relations, and individual and collective rape is oftentimes a product of such relations. 'From head to toe, her body has turned into openings for death to penetrate! . . . Her sons are cutting whatever they can of her flesh to hang on the walls of their houses as a sign of longing. Their bodies are stuffed in her womb, a rape of them and her.' Al-Asheq blames the military that sold whatever it could of their flesh and land. It started wars, gained their loss and built a wasteland. 'That is when our rape began.' Describing the rape of a Yazidi woman in Sinjar, he writes: 'People will say that she turned into a fighter because of me [Birûsk]. To them I say, "We never chose to fight. We are the merciful children of the first murderer." '

Al-Asheq's depictions of masculinity do not shy away from questioning what it means to 'be a "man" or a "hero"': 'There is no hero on that land sown with injustice and war. There is no hero there except for death, standing victorious as it awaits your flesh.' In this description, 'Rojenda carries her rifle and attacks death like a lioness. She shoots quickly as she cries. She shoots and cries and calls out his living name, yearning for him. She was trying to burn the earth for no reason other than fighting darkness and its men, to bring the myth of "the sun granting life" to fruition.'

The collection is full of unspeakable forms of violence but also of love and playfulness. This duality of life/death, past/present, real/imagined, light/darkness, individual/ collective, love/revenge, joy/pain, hope/despair, beauty/ ugliness weaves in and out of each of the seventeen texts. Describing his lover, Al-Asheq says, 'I know she cares about what is going on in Syria. Yet, she is more concerned with this refugee who snatched back his wonder from the mouth of death after seeing her.' In 'The Seller of Love and Their Bed', he writes of his relation to his bed: 'I'm stuck in bed, living in it as if it were my mother's womb . . . A multipurpose bed, square. It substituted for a writing table for a long time and witnessed romantic battles between me and my imagination. It drinks coffee with me in the morning and eats the meals I conjure up. The bed's addicted to smoking. It knows many names that have never got near it.'

Longing and yearning define past and present relations. They are what kill you yet keep you alive. Longing in this context 'is darker than kohl! It is a mother's voice to her child. The voice of a pained heart, the wind and a breeze. It is the sound of lute when strummed, the sound of an arrow when it's nocked. It is the sound of missing someone.' It is a voice, 'and I have lost mine—if I ever had one at all . . . I will scream with all the cowardice I had when I ran away and emigrated, with all my pain as if I were a woman just like her and the same thing happened to me.'

Al-Asheq wonders whether death could clear some space for life, and whether the loss of memory is the only salvation for going back to the day his mother gave birth to him. He describes it as a pilgrimage to repent for the pain, to purify all the corpses that paint the walls of his dreams in red and black. Writing of the destruction of the Yarmouk Refugee Camp, he traces the second displacement of Palestinians from Syria: 'They left the way they had over sixty years ago . . . They only left what they could not carry. They left houses heavy with memories. They left streets that ate pieces of their feet. They left clothes that carry their smell and guard it under ashes . . . They left the names themselves: Haifa, Jerusalem, Carmel, Al-Qastal, Al-Tira, Lubya, Safad.' They carried 'scars matching the number of people in the camp.' He adds that these sad, ugly stories have their place: 'Without them, the beautiful, uplifting ones would have no taste. They build the myth of their beauty on the ugliness of others.'

The collection ends with a piece titled 'Ever Since I Did Not Die'. It encompasses the book and forms its title, beginning and end: 'Ever since I did not die, I've become a mouse and I chomp on borrowed time. I make a space out of every corner and peel off the covers of books before I am stuck in the trap of fear. I get lost among the pillars of monumental churches looking for a familiar face not swallowed by forgetting.' He recognizes that he was born when he did not die. He carries migrations whose pain his passport endured for an insanity that is still without end. He traces four stones that lost their way to falling, and admits that they missed his head which had got rid of all that came before: 'One stone fell, broken with a childhood I never noticed. Another hung the women of before-death from their breasts and crashed down. Another broke through superstitions about God, his masculinity and the stories of a Palestinian grandmother running away from a defeat she rejects and fights against with delusions. The last one fell, and I noticed a broken smile saying, "You are my lipstick." '

A ticking clock keeps track of time, and of the many times he did not die. 'The first is in a land I didn't choose. The second is in a prison that opened a door to the sun through a sewage pipe. The third is in a lap that taught me not to give up. The fourth is in the lap that lost my warmth. The fifth is in the window of realization about how I survived, how I drove death into exile and threw it away.' Al-Asheq resists death through shoving poetry, melted in the fire of love, into death's ears to wipe its memory. Then he bites its ears so it will never return.

Ever since he did not die he started to taste beauty. Al-Asheq opens war's door, the chapter of fear, and sinks further into the hatred of heroism. Ever since he did not die he lost his identity. He does not care much if he carries one or it carries him! He wonders how he could confirm the image of a homeland he refuses. Al-Asheq gets drunk on love as if he did not die, as if he were a 'minaret singing songs of love for a simple God who does not swing a stick or bless the water'. He writes about death, not life. 'You don't write about life, you live it!' He ends by admitting to vulnerability and fear. Fear, the most 'honest feeling I've known and a sincere friend who has accompanied me for a long time without quarrel or estrangement. That is why I did not die. If I had, I would have become a hero, but I don't find anything deserving in heroism.' Al-Asheq is leaving us with his writing and what it took for him to survive. His survival is part of ours with all the responsibilities entailed in that. Or, as put by Audre Lorde:

> So it is better to speak
> remembering
> we were never meant to survive.[2]

*

Special thanks to Levi Thompson for his valuable editorial help; to Tuesday Carson, a senior at Denison University, for reviewing the manuscript; and to the team at Seagull Books. This translation was made possible through a grant from the Denison University Research Fund.

---

2 Audre Lorde, 'A Litany for Survival', *The Collected Poems of Audre Lorde (1978)*. Available at: https://www.poetryfoundation.org/ poems/ 147275/a-litany-for-survival

Preface

I gathered these texts like someone collecting body parts. Here are the pieces of my body, haphazardly brought together in a paper bag. This randomness of body parts is real in its destruction. Bloody at times, violent, honest, imaginary, personal. It looks like me with all my madness and sickness, how the revolution made me grow, what the war broke inside me and what exile chipped away.

I have no head, no name, no identity. I gathered these pieces while fully believing that reality needs me to be a writer more than a poet. All that is emotional is not poetry, what does not belong to music is not poetry and the ugliness surrounding us hurts poetry. We could say that this is just a collection of texts, texts that could bear a name. Call them what you like. I tried, without having decided beforehand, to make the ugly beautiful and to put on layers of mascara to make it seem what they call 'creative'. When I wrote these pieces, I did not think they would be collected in a book, turned into a testimony or published in any certain form. Let us save this collection from classification as it has already suffered enough cruelty at the hands of its author.

Escaping from Paradise

Suitcases stuffed with fear. Clothes smelling of disappointment. Shoes for amputated feet. Pictures of a family that no longer exists. Faces thin except for their fury. Eyes spouting dry salt. Mouths without throats screaming, throats cut out and left behind. Ears that know only the music of funerals and the sound of death. Death has two sounds: the first is explosions, screaming and the like. The second: silence. Silence is the sound of death intensified. Eyes that only see destruction, worlds no longer there, blood more than air and air shot through with the ashes of burnt bodies. The tent is waiting, the tent that is Judgement Day. Only a few go to tents that are less deadly. The rest go to tents of Hell. Angels circle them wearing uniforms with blue logos, and God, as usual, does not show up. There are no rivers here except those hung in the memory of the massacre. The *houris* feast on dirt. Children circle, begging for water. The sand the children used to love turned into burning embers and ice.

Minutes before the Resurrection, the dead-alive walked across the crooked path towards a lesser death. The soldiers shoved them, drove them, robbed them. 'Who is your God?' they asked each one, 'What is your religion? What is your book?' Rifle butts struck him. He screamed a scream the whole universe heard, except for three: God; the international community; and his people. The wounded rise up like waves before they fall again. They are resurrected, only to be thrown again into the hell that is the tent for seventy more years. There is no power for them, surrounded with nothing but desert and their own skin. A call rings out in the market for the half-dead who used to be half-gods. Half of them were crucified while the other half remained a banner of thirst, a museum of hunger, a public square of ugliness. Paradise is offered to the beautiful women for the sake of death's face. They are sold as fearful leftover goods. Only those who sold profited!

An hour before Resurrection, the murderer's child was wearing a military uniform and carrying a plastic rifle. He shot the television screen, and a barrel bomb fell somewhere far off. He laughs, shoots, a rocket takes off and vacuum bombs fall. He shoots, and his army opens windows in our bodies. He shoots for six days and rests on the seventh. The tireless murderer keeps going without slumbering. He laughs like the sky but does not cry like it. Before Resurrection, no one was free except those in prison. No one was alive except those who died free. Before, fear was nothingness, and darkness filled the face of existence. Before . . . the son of God became a God, he ploughed people's faces and ate their hearts. They were in pain, screaming. He killed them and gave a speech over the remains of their bodies, terrifying those who cut out their tongues and ripped out their throats to keep from screaming. 'My children,' he said, 'I ate your hearts to save you from pain, and you ate your tongues to do the same!'

Before, the military occupied people's minds and lands. Death attacked like morning does. Life became death and death life. The military sold whatever they could of our flesh and land. They started wars and gained our loss. They got stronger as we got weaker. They forced our necks to bend. They fucked our faces and started to build a wasteland. That is when our rape began.

A few days before (*Al-Ba'th*), life was more beautiful!

The Refugee and the Other,
the Other Refugee

War is vast. It reaches across the horizon, loftier and older than peace. Killing came before war, but it might also be that refuge preceded war. It got attached to war like a child holding on to its mother's dress with one hand, the other waving to those it does not know. The refugee: a flute weeping over its original image before there was a camp. The camp: ginger on the back of humanity's infected throat. The camp is necessary, sometimes, for remembering that the lands across the river dropped off the face of the map when we weren't looking. The map: geography on paper, its borders drawn by the tank and the mortar shell for eternity. The mortar: a tiny cosmic explosion that re-arranges habitats by the whims of whoever launches it. One night, the mortar launcher awakened superstition from its sleep and dragged it away with an F-16 saying, 'I cannot exist . . . unless there is a refugee.'

Is it our instinct to always blame the victim? Is it cus-tomary for the victim to keep playing this role even after the decided time has passed? The victim might even like it and consider it a privilege. That way the Other—but not every Other—will have reason to regard the victim as a scapegoat. The victim sees the Other as a potential enemy, a current friend who is ready to attack at any moment. This has become an essential existential component of the dualities of the universe that are always, as they say, subject to unilateral rule. Good is sometimes evil, and wrong is right. A supporter could be an opponent on another side, and night might be day. The Other is not an Other elsewhere. 'There' is only 'there' here. Likewise, the refugee could become the Other someday, and responds to another who has become a refugee just like them. Dualities are suspended in conflict and change. Absolute unilateralism lies at the root of this conflict as creator and caretaker and is one of the main reasons for its persistence.

The Other asks the long-time refugee, 'Do the people in the camp really live in tents?' The refugee doesn't respond. Instead, the refugee camp responds, 'Nothing has anything to do with its name!'

How?

The tents tricked time and stretched their necks until they blocked out the sun. People came to me for pilgrimage from every corner of the earth. They were crowded, since the 'earth was without form, and void; and darkness was upon the face of the deep'.

So, why are you still called a 'camp'?

How would the Other recognize me if I were to change my name?

The Other branded them and marked their pictures in red: 'You have no place here in the long run.' Others contributed by adding features in bright oil on their foreheads, so the Other named them. They liked the new name—at least, they liked it until it didn't please them any longer. It became as ordinary as death in this vast war. The Other did not tell them anything. They did not know the place or the time when yet another Other would rename them. They made a point of not asking. Perhaps fewer questions mean less pain.

One of them says, 'I'm a refugee who was born here, the son of a refugee who was born here. We know nothing but "here". Fifty years of my dad living "here" were not enough to change what he was called. My mother's nationality wasn't enough for me to change what I'm called! That's why I hate children—my children, not those of others—because I do not want them to be refugees.' He does not want them to be like him: different! Even in revolution, the Other wins when he turns those who are alike into Others from themselves.

The refugee opens the door of his tent (his palace) to the Other (the non-refugee). The Other becomes part of this camp that was destroyed except for its name. The Other grows up saying, 'I am from there,' and the refugee says, 'I am from "here" and from another "there". I am from my temporary "here", and my original "there" until the day I return!' Should things get hard one day, the Other will scream in the face of the refugee, 'You are not from "here". You are from "there". You and your camp are in the "here" that belongs to me, so leave!'

So, he leaves, and not much leaves with him. When he remains, nothing will be left of him. The fiasco does not stop here. Indeed, the Other, who used to be a brother, becomes an informant, an enemy. The refugee goes back to repeating the story and playing the role of the victim. The victim is another victim, and the criminal is, of course, an Other!

Everything changes. Nothing remains fixed except for the refugee. Even a temporary homeland becomes a prison, borders surrounded with barbed wire tightly connected to the sea on one side, and to stolen electrical lines on the other. This homeland-prison becomes more merciful than the neighbour-prison. The next camp becomes a real, not metaphorical, prison. The escapee becomes a wanted man, accused of infiltrating paradise. They are tossed into the hell of war seventy times. He ages like fruit. The newspapers sleep on his story through day and night. The people of the land, the sky, and those in-between ignore him because of a royal decree.

Several long-time refugees were rescued along with some Others. They sang the anthem of death to sea and land. The weather picked up, and only those who were already buried could be saved without the camp. The partners of refugee and tent were separated, but they were allowed to return if the Other approved. The Others were called refugees. The long-time refugees are now called 'without'. This is not about nothingness or nihilism but about a death verdict. He carried many names, as many as his migrations. They put them all to death with another Universal Declaration. The 'without' remained nameless, just like they will always be!

With this separation and change in the structure of dualities, some refugees received a nationality and became citizens. They might not want to admit that they are half-citizens or second-class citizens. The original defence mechanism of denial always wins out over confirmation. Having gained their nationality, they were considered to be part of the Other, and they practiced their Otherness on Others. Whenever war smiled, they screamed at them. As they were transformed, they forgot their past: 'O Refugees!'

This is how one refugee killed another when the first became an Other. The second had to hold onto the title to avoid turning into nothing.

I Raise Your Body
as a Banner of Horror
and Disappointment

The wound is greater. The hand stretching from one shoulder to another has lost its shadow. The eyes dare not see. Sadness insists on repeating the effects of the massacre. Only blood keeps us together. A body without a soul, a soul without wings, children without parents, mothers without wombs and a memory unable to bear anything but pain. The sky did not stop performing the role of a murderer. Earth fell in love with injustice. The river is a pre-confession that water can move. The walls are stones erected despite wanting to break their will. Glass is the attempt of a wall to reveal a secret. When blood speaks, everything goes silent. Only blood keeps us together. Your blood disappeared from your face. I did not recognize you when you stood in front of me. Blood disappeared from your hands. I did not see them waving, and they did not reach out to shake hands with my fear. It disappeared from your heart, which did not jump with surprise at the sight of my long beard. Your blood disappeared. It ran between us, which is why you did not hear my screams and wailing!

Maybe you did not feel how I carried you anew after our separation, how your blood spoke and how I sank in your water as I used to, even though its colour had changed. 'I know this face,' I say, then I deny knowing it. I howl like a dog whose ear they cut off and made him eat. Then I go mute and turn into a murderer. I know your smell. I deny it and flee. I return. I embrace you. I call out to you, and I cry. I go mad. I see you flying over defeated countries. I carry the irritability of a bullet, the depravity of a bomb. I leave naked wearing only a stolen helmet. I fill the sky with rotten shots given to us to make our suicide easier. I raise your body as a banner of horror and disappointment. As I fall, I call out, 'It's still raining blood!'

Get up, run away from all my questions, or answer me! Your silence means my victory. I am the darkness that is all you can see. Do you like the white shroud now? Don't stand up against my questions like a ruin! Get up, and desert me again. Leave! Take whatever you want and get out of your bleeding body. O tent, betraying land, return to the refugee! Ration stamps don't make up for land. Solitude is a disease I cherish. The cold is crueller, the longing heavier. I embrace a corpse, my corpse. I get good at telling secrets and waving to memory. I dance like someone touched by a jinn. I stare into the distance for a long time. I wait for a gesture, a sign, a miracle . . . and a smile!

Two different bodies. One body and another do not get together except to part. In the crowd, I just see an old face, a waist I know everything about. A hand waving in silence. These features could belong to someone I know. Is the sea capable of all of this? Or is it the war? They have the same letters, but the form is different!

Who gave them these names? Who marked me with blackness? Who grew my beard? Who told the strangers about my privates? Who stole my whiteness, hid it away and then presented it to her in the shape of a shroud?

I scream. My intestines fall out. We feed our flesh to Death as a banquet. We pour blood onto the asphalt. He might not appreciate its value, but I do. She might not appreciate its value, but I do. Then again, I might not, so I become long, dark, without a shadow, like a hand stretching from her shoulder to mine. Here . . . in this old and repeated moment they call a 'massacre', I will be happy for every laugh that goes on after I die.

How I Know the Cell

I know myself when I start breathing in a woman, her memory, her smell, and the perfume of words that opens wide the door of her mouth, the way children, their class having finished at the bell's ring, scream with joy. I know myself when my air becomes my woman. I start defending my chest, smoking tobacco. I inhale the smoke and hold it in my lungs to take up more space on account of the woman I'm breathing. I hold it in, and I exhale a breath that's empty except for her image. I puff her out in a portrait of smoke.

I know that I defend my freedom in front of a prison shaped like a woman. The iron bars are a rib cage made from soft bones. The prison's floor is a body I cannot get enough of. The smell of prison is that of my decomposing body, surrendered to her madness. Prisons have no smell. They stink of the decomposition of those who went mad, those who gave in to the impossibility of leaving. Darkness is her hair, my eyes and my lungs. The clink of iron is the clashing of memory when it bumps into the wall of reality. Time doesn't exist in the cell, doesn't exist with her. Thinking about it means a certain suicide. Whoever has been in prison will most likely become claustrophobic and open up whatever they can to take her for a trip in the fresh air. He will tell her about the sky and ability of colours to spread life, about the beauty of running towards the void and about his hatred of all cement walls and fortified-iron windows. He will eat ten irregular meals a day and pee every five minutes. He will pee everywhere, behind every tree and on any wall. He will smoke more than he sleeps, and if he wanted to sleep, he will only do so with the wind blowing through open windows, the lights on, and loud music playing. He will hang clocks all over the place, each marking the time of a different city. If walls are absolutely necessary, he will make one in the shape of a huge calendar, another into an aquarium, a third into a television or a mirror and a fourth into a library. He will cover the floor with a green carpet like the ones used for sports fields. The window will become his altar. Unless he has to, he won't live below the fourth floor.

I know myself. I know that smoking is like writing diaries of fear. Intense accounts that resemble a dark cloud. I try to make the ugly beautiful with language, but gloomy thoughts suffocate me. I become a news broadcast. The news has no language. Language is nothing but a scam to document and judge events. I ask my German-Palestinian friend who specializes in speech therapy about who invented language.

'God. The Old Testament says that people long ago spoke a single ur-language. When they first thought about building, they tried to build a tower that could bring them to the sky. They were about to get there. When God saw them ascending, God created languages, and made each one of them speak a different language. They quarrelled and could not reach an understanding, so they destroyed the tower!'

I know myself. I have no language other than what I write. Uttering words is a privilege I do not want to have. I used to say what I wanted to the wall that wore down my fingernails. I used to scream at the cold to warm myself with anger. I would sing to my imagination until I became intoxicated. The enemies I have now are the ones I got to know before. Don't you ever mention olives and boiled potatoes in front of me, or I'll become a monster.

The woman is my prison. However pretty the prison, it is still a prison. I escaped from prison once, and we parted ways peacefully in the second one. It threw me up many times to get rid of me. I will stay like this until I find what I want . . . the freedom woman.

*The Fighter
Stripped of Her Braids*

The writer called me 'Rojenda' because he didn't know my name. If he had asked, I would have told him that I'm a woman without braids. A young girl who remembers nothing but death. A fighter holding back all my tears, born in Sinjar and older than its massacre. I carry blood revenge on my chest, with his picture on a golden chain. A picture showing all his features and taken before the massacre, the massacre that produced blood revenge like an unwanted fetus. I'm loyal to it now. My name has disappeared. All that remains are my story, my braids and my revenge. His name has disappeared. All that remains are his picture and a stone that says, 'Here he lives in your soul.' His name has disappeared so the writer called him Birûsk. If he had asked, I would have told him that he was an awe-inspiring man who stopped for nothing less than life, a smile that went silent and vanished under the dirt far too early. A heart fluttering with love songs who made the *buzuq* a prayer to the sun. Two hands playing with my hair and lifting up my braids with the fragrance of cinnamon.

Let us assume that my name is Rojenda. In Kurmanji, it means 'the sun gives life', Rojenda, who cut her braids and tied them to a tombstone as an identity. Here is where Birûsk's body rests, his soul lives within me. Rojenda is now two souls for two lovers. One of them was killed and the other is seeking blood revenge. One murdered and the other a murderer in the making, or maybe she too will be murdered.

I left my braid on top of a stone under the sun so that the sun can grant life to those darkness had killed. Birûsk means a meteor swallowed by a monster. It turned him into a story and left me to mourn, a fighter with short hair.

* * *

You can call me Birûsk, a meteor coming from the sun in order to save the earth from blood. Another prophet killed because he does not resemble other people. I was planning to take Rojenda to a city that hasn't changed its name yet. When I decided to infiltrate the night, its darkness swallowed me up. I used to burn so I can see, but in the end, I turned into ashes buried in the dirt, which left me nothing except for the tombstone and her braids that I breathed in. People will say that she turned into a fighter because of me. To them I say, 'We never chose to fight. We are the merciful children of the first murderer. We wanted to live a life full of love under the sun, but the state hates the sun.

By "state", I mean all our nations that could be called by such a name, or the ones that falsely called themselves so.'

* * *

My dear Birûsk, I know that you do not like killing. I know that you open your tender chest to life in order to make a forest out of love. I know that you will rest more if I were to flee and save myself. I will never rest until I get revenge for you. Revenge is the last song of justice, and if I am killed, I will return to you anew.

* * *

My love, Rojenda, do not die. Love life as I loved it and open the door to a smile so that the wolves of the night run away, and cry. Don't run away from your tears. Crying is the most important and distinctive part of being human. Whoever tries to run away from tears or pass them along to others is a liar, pretending that the trees, horses, and birds are crying instead. He runs from his solitude to become something else, so wait until your braids grow again, and live crying as much as you can.

* * *

Rojenda carries her rifle and attacks death like a lioness. She shoots quickly as she cries. She shoots and cries and calls out his living name, yearning for him. She was trying to burn the earth for no reason other than fighting darkness and its men, to bring the myth of 'the sun granting life' to fruition. As she attacks, she is surrounded by a halo of light and fire. Darkness will not swallow the light of the sun or the meteor's fire this time. Rojenda successfully pleads her case in the face of death. She peels night off her body and dances with life in her steps. Birûsk watches his myth grunting, crying, fighting, and the fragrance of cinnamon from the braids fills his grave. All I know of this Yezidi woman is the image of her braids on a stone in Sinjar. She will one day affirm both his name and hers. Only then will the text return to its fighting imagination.

The Village Crocheter

The teacher, seduced by his student, was gathering up his palms from her village face. He carried two ages in addition to hers and placed them between her eyes so he could kiss her. No one was around. It was like a late-night private lesson on love. The place was nearly empty, and darkness surrounded the sky and earth. The distance between them extended from the mountains of Ammon to the most handsome king of the world's rivers. Maro, the crocheter, exhales the breath of her desire in his direction. He bellows, the river roars and the bed shakes.

She tended to the cherry tree so it would produce songs and poems. She gathered prose from the edges of the poem and wore it like jewellery on her neck. She wanted her neck to be a playground for his lips. His lips tried to reach the white behind her earlobe that resembled him and circled her shoulders. He would nuzzle his pain with her exaggerated, intoxicating shiver as if it was the last piece of marijuana he would spark up before disappearing.

The crocheter, with the features of south Damascus peasants, opens the way for her eyebrows to be completely free. She carries the cotton fields on her round cheeks and buries them in cherries. Cherries dotted with moles left by Damascus, a birthmark that will remain should Damascus disappear. She would leave the techniques of narrative and poetry that he taught her glowing like red markers on her face and sweat dripping to her belly button. Maro resists when the straps of her green camisole start to slip in the blast. The cherry tree might need to burn to release its trunk from all this heavy green! The corn fields crowning her head had to conceal the eyes of the silent leopard, alert and waiting for his prey. 'There are no wild animals here,' he tells himself. 'Take that step and burn the place with fire. Don't worry about the features of the leopard. It's just a village cat that's used to hunting sparrows.'

'Don't dye your hair blond!' says her mother. The teacher agrees. The young girl thinks it's just good guardianship. The lesson goes back to being a lesson, and she goes back to acting like a leopard. The place seems to get narrower and narrower, and the walls close on their solitude. The sky closes its eyes, and cherry cheeks become jugs of vintage wine. Darkness is exposed in the white of her shivering body, and the son of exile is scared of becoming a corpse. He attacks, but the cat remains hidden inside him. She puts her head on his shoulder and cries.

The eyes of the informants were closed. They waved to these eyes with pity. The informant could have stopped if he was able to live securely. Security is a fortress known only to the crocheter. It extended from the teacher's armpit to his chest hair that stops at the bottom of his neglected beard. That is where the young girl had set up her swing, far away from the sounds of war silenced by his chest. She would listen to his heartbeat like someone waiting for the bomb that ends an Oriental jazz party. 'Music is the source,' he used to say. He sighed with a beat hidden by the clarinet player, a tune that flies off and then returns to him like a flock of pigeons roaming over the city on their way home. They were outside the borders of war, but it remained inside them. Silence was a lifeline, a banner of peace that assured them that the battles had stopped, leaving nothing behind. The cherry tree was in a pot without dirt because wool had abandoned the text and created a footnote in their image. The teacher held to his roots, had to admit that the colours of crochet are much more beautiful than the colour of a real cherry tree.

Maro slept. She said goodbye to the night the way she usually did. 'May we awaken with a poem.' Morning was so close that the son of exile travelled to her bed to see the white that loosened the straps of the green camisole. He dipped a piece of sweating cherry and it brought forth a lemon, squeezed out on a body splashed with joy. He made it to her bed, but he caught her just as she put on her clothes and left!

I Do Not Want to
Fall in Love with Her

I do not want to love her, so I will write a lot about her. I will talk about her to every cigarette I smoke. When the cigarette dissolves into the world of ashes, it will take her secret to every dead person I've known or will know, to every face of fear, to every piece of clothing I will wear when I want to meet her, to every woman who passes my way and sees how I train my face to smile for her. I will make her famous, and I hate famous people. I will do my utmost to make her recognize how I substitute three letters that have no meaning on their own in her beautiful name.

'H' – 'e' – 'r', I will write about her!

This 'her', who has green eyes like this city, takes me in whenever she feels bored. She roams the streets, the bars and the Arab stores with me whenever her lover neglects her. Lately, I have not been able to immediately understand what she is saying as I am in a different world most of the time. The world: her mouth. The Other: a pillar of civilizations battling against history, refusing to fall apart, remaining white only to give her a charming smile. I always try to count our inheritance of the world's moles on our faces and bodies. She doesn't care about that because peasants rise above the luxury of city-dwellers. The golden ring that pierces her right nostril and turns like a golden swing for an impetuous baby sometimes turns her into an amusement park, or into an umbilical cord stretching back from the last love story he lived in a previous life to the first cell the universe knew after non-existence.

I cannot believe that the scar sitting under her left eye like a dimple is an injury, the result of falling off a bicycle sometime in her childhood. I will always try to fight with the common people, (police), beggars, and dogs, so I can get a scar like hers.

I do not love her.

I say it to myself, adding that I love her presence in the midst of my solitude. I love our silence when we hide what we are thinking as we usually do, when we lose track of time. I love to see her. I left two books about war and death, books I was about to finish so I could instead concentrate on thinking about her like a teenager would! I love that I am writing for the first time about something beautiful in the midst of all this ugliness, like a womb from which I have not yet been born. I love how I care about the shape of her fingers, the colour of her nails, her voice, and her constant attempts to conceal her happiness in what I say to her.

I know she cares about what is going on in Syria. Yet, she is more concerned with this refugee who snatched back his wonder from the mouth of death after seeing her. He changed his route at one in the morning and missed his bus because he saw her sitting at the train station. He pretended to be lost so he could find a reason to start a conversation with her and go somewhere else! He revealed all his secrets before he got drunk. He got drunk anyway after drinking just a little, and left her to go to someone else! She is interested in this child who is older than her by three years, two catastrophes, three displacements, two imprisonments, three states, two continents; someone stateless with no passport!

She is beautiful, the way I drew her in my imagination twenty years ago, a girl for my small dreams. Beautiful only when we are together or maybe the pictures do not do her justice! It could be that the refugee is used to raising the ceiling of his madness to compensate for his compounding losses. She is beautiful yet her behind is not curvy, and her breasts are not tight. I still do not know their size since I don't know for sure if she wore a bra whenever we met. Her toes are ordinary, and the distance between her feet and behind is not long. As a side note, I've changed my mind about the beauty of tall women since I came to Germany because I've become a short person myself! My mouth stuck to her neck during the first and last real embrace between us when I was drunk. It was the most beautiful place I have put a poem since I learnt how to write!

She's smart. She knows how to pull words out of my heart and follow them through my insides until I say them.

Then she smiles. She's a sneaky one who makes it easy for me to step towards the carrot hanging in front of the donkey's head in the schoolbook. That's when I discovered how difficult, complicated, and close to impossible the task really is.

She does not love me either, and she does not love him. She loves how two people from different worlds hover over her. But she herself hovers over one and follows the other who is hungrier for her. She throws him a piece of biscuit dipped in her saliva and goes away!

Let us agree on God and differ on our favourite beer and who will pay the bill. Let us fight each time over how small her bladder is, and how she always needs to pee behind a tree because she does not want to pay to pee in one of the stores! Let us boycott each other debating over any food that contains animal products, and part in peace when we have something to say about our favourite music. Let us fight a war of endless destruction over my hate for children and dogs and her love for them! Most importantly, I started to feel. I was starting to fall in love with (her). I (fall) for one exact minute, as love is almost like falling from freedom against every height, rising up, and soaring. Even if your stupid heart felt like flying whenever you remembered her name, and since I realize that I've started to fall, I've been writing about her until this very word.

I keep following my fall into nothing, and from here— from the last lost point—I talk to you, and keep on falling!

The Test of Longing

'Where are you from?' I answer without hesitation. I know her name by heart unlike the names of my other lovers whom I deserted and who deserted me. She is the only one whose name I don't get confused, the only one where there is no evidence of her betrayal, or mine. I wish with everything that makes me a man that, if I were completely female, I would not fall in love with her. I memorized the route for her migration and mine on the back of my wound. I kept myself away from her with all my manhood after she was raped in the name of honour because I was afraid, or perhaps to hold on to her virgin image in my mind!

I peel my fear, one image after another. I recall the scene of the crime, one scream after another. Blood on her face, on my hands, on the sky that watches collective rape and smiles. Males from different nationalities and species, animals, half-gods, sick gods whose sacrifices are the cracks of our smiles, humans with animal heads, animals with human heads, soldiers, soldiers, soldiers, common uniforms, turbans covering genitals, rifles growing out of testicles, clothes torn by desire, a one-sided low-life desire, a wrestling match for a crowd practicing how to masturbate while screaming—screaming, because it's impossible for them to clap!

I test out longing. I try to remember. All I can see is blood. The streets that I am addicted to are dark red. The trees burnt themselves in mourning, spread their ashes to conceal the smell of corpses. The water is red. Her face drowns in his blood. Her ears are cut off. Her nose is bleeding. Her breast is pierced with a bayonet. Her belly button is torn open and her guts are a noose from which she alone hangs. Cigarettes put out on her skin. Tyrant's slogans written on her neck with blood. The 'Allahu Akbar!' of an elder trying to beat the tyrant to get to her mouth. From head to toe, her body has turned into openings for death to penetrate!

I try once more! Houses disappear. Dust accumulates as the rubble grows. I can clearly see one of them carrying a sharp instrument and beginning to pluck her eyelashes. He bites them together with her eyelids. Her sons are cutting whatever they can of her flesh to hang on the walls of their houses as a sign of longing. I start the test again. I search for the faces of the ones I love. I see them as bodies without heads. Their bodies are stuffed in her womb, a rape of them and her. Farms shaped like shrouds, minarets without heads, churches without crosses, women who have lost their femininity, men completely defeated, children who know nothing of childhood except its name, and the murderers . . . only the murderers dance. They fuck each other on top of her body!

I long . . . I long for nothing else the way I long to be in her lap. I shrug it off, running away from the dream. I've tried to stay away from music ever since we parted ways. Music disgraces the work of longing. I keep away from poetry because it has the same fragrance as her body. I avoid writing since it comes out like shed blood. I walk alone having completely lost my memory, thirsting to forget. I travel as far away as the scattered ashes of a dead body, and I die like someone who goes on living without her!

Hanin, the Arabic word for 'longing', doesn't come from the same place as *henna*. Longing is darker than kohl! It is a mother's voice to her child. The voice of a pained heart, the wind and a breeze. It is the sound of a lute when strummed, the sound of an arrow when it's nocked. It is the sound of missing someone. Longing is a voice, and I have lost mine—if I ever had one at all. I won't try to speak again, repeat or call out. I will scream out from all the pain of the crime, the blood's thirst for blood, the escapee's fear of death, the thirst of someone drowning in the sea, the hunger of someone abandoned in a tent. I will scream with all my anger, revenge, fire, blasphemy and hatred. I will scream with all the cowardice I had when I ran away and emigrated, with all my pain as if I were a woman just like her and the same thing happened to me. I will scream, 'If only she had died!'

We Finally Meet

We did not meet much after that. I used to meet her in my imagination and draw birds kissing each other on her body, some spikes of grain belly dancing, glass walls not revealing what's inside them, not because of some special technical power but because everything outside them is empty. I used to follow the movement of her pupils with a mother's caution and play with her hair like a lover afraid of what's to come. I used to hang her hand around my neck and take her to faraway lands she didn't know so she couldn't escape. I don't recognize her in order not to escape. I used to pull her close to my chest for her smell to stick to my clothes. I would break the silence with a question that has not been asked, and come back to stretch clouds under her feet, tickling her dream of coming down. She said that she is afraid of heights. I did not dare admit that. I said, 'I am your land, your country, your fence, your crystal wall, your first thought of safety. I am your future favorite song, a tree full of children playing with your smile. I am an old story only your tongue can tell, the same tongue that shot a bullet into my ear when it said, timidly, "No."'

We did not meet much after that. We used to make a date, but our sly plan for a meeting would fail. The room, which was accustomed to chaos, would panic from the sudden order. It prepared itself for candles that were never lit. The windows could feel happiness inside themselves as cigarettes, frozen in place, suffocated them. I used to say farewell to the dust the way I said goodbye to a secret lover when my mother came home. Whenever we failed to meet, I would go out, hating all that had been tidied up for someone who did not show up. I look for her. I do not look at single girls. I thought she did not come because she was with him. I sneak a peek at couples hugging and kissing. I run to the empty corners of the deserted city, forgetting that they might meet at a house—something I'm unaccustomed to. Then I sit under her window until late at night, except she doesn't come. I believe the story about her trip, but I cannot imagine her sleeping at his house.

Finally, we met again, for the last time; a farewell that spans the life of a foetus. I spread out all the waiting I had done, collecting up the smiles of a life I never lived. Funny stories, discussions about the history of animal welfare— a long debate, and answers to the questions I expected her to ask in order to keep the date going. I stood by the window hours before our date, waiting for her arrival which would surely be delayed. I saw how she passed through the street walking slowly, how she walks even more slowly as she plays with the children and smiles at them. She finally entered, we spoke a little about her trip, then silence reigned.

She went off travelling, waved with one hand without turning it. She smiled without moving her lips. She didn't say: I love you. She didn't say: wait for me. She hid my body's heat in a cup she didn't finish because it wasn't cold enough. She pretended to be interested in the jazz music I prepared for our final date. She did not ask about the lit candles. Instead, with a sly smile, she asked me, 'Is your house always this clean and tidy, or is it because you invited me over?'

Borrowing

There were only songs between us. We borrowed voices foreign to our throats, memories that refused to knock on the doors of our past. We borrowed smells of other bodies, and smiles from television scenes from our childhood. We learnt these songs from our teachers, both women and men. We saw them singing them to one another. We loved the songs the way they sang them. When we heard the original versions, they seemed out of tune. Although we never loved our teachers, we would grudgingly eat the cheese and *za'tar* sandwiches our mothers prepared for school trips while they were barbecuing meat and making tabbouleh. They would make us collect branches to light the fire of their feast and our desires.

Songs are our first image of joy. This was not the case later on. We still try to sing the songs in their voices while searching for happiness: the green plain, suitcases scattered like light corpses, a Scania bus with plastic bunches of grapes hanging from its roof. Its gel seats carved in the shape of behinds that got used to sitting in them for long periods of time, the drum, the colours of the female teachers' ugly faces, the seductive masculine looks. The smell of the male teachers' sweat mixed with the female teachers' cheap perfume. Our own smells, like that of a herd of sheep which had stood in one place for a whole month. Our chats about the neighbourhood girls and school. Our fathers' repeated sentences and the curses that moved from mouth to mouth. You can summarize all these crimes in songs!

I'm looking for happiness, not love. I stumble onto her body. I pull from her patriarchy into the femininity of my words, and poetry comes out. I borrow the memory of the teacher and put on a child's troublemaking. I fall under an old chair sneaking around the way she shakes her leg. I lift my head up to see her biting her nails. I exit from my borrowed memory into imagination. I throw millions of me into a sperm bank, and I wait a little for them to grow and resemble her. I look for them in foreign streets. The same eyes with blonde hair. The same mouth with a new skin colour. The laugh that echoes my teacher's on a body two teachers high, one carrying the other so they can climb a tree and take a funny picture. I see my face on her body—the same face the mirror told me about. I thought it was my own. I am full of joy. I run. I scream. I attack. I hug this creature divided by a borrowed motherhood and get slapped in the face!

She is looking for love. She opens the door to a poem, leaving it ajar so I can come in. She forgets an apostrophe on purpose knowing that it will provoke me. She delves into communicating with the unknown. She likes it when I am anonymous, so she can see my heart break as I look into the eyes of people unable to speak:

'This is me! I am the intended one as ugly as I may be. I am mentioned even if I am nothing!'

No one can hear what is on my mind. I leave happiness and look for love. I drown, fall, get jealous, cry, isolate myself. I walk in the street talking with her absence. I sing for her. The songs are no longer songs of happiness. They are the songs of teenagers crashing into loss. I borrow anew a smile and lipstick on a shirt collar that is not mine. I steal a bank card from my foreign girlfriend. I sit at the restaurant, looking for a green plain, tabbouleh and some barbecued meat. I ride a Scania bus from a distant European town to there—there, where the first images of the songs are, so I can teach the children how to sing!

The
Ones
I've Killed
So Far

For Elias Sem'aan

I confess. I killed them all, each in a different way. The first was my father. I brought him into a dark room so I wouldn't see his face. I took off his glasses so I wouldn't hurt my hand. I tied him to the ground and spread his legs. I started beating his testicles with my hands, feet and a heavy stick until I killed him. I killed him more than once. I did it again for every time he used to hit me hard and say, 'You dog! I peed you! You think you can talk back to me!?'

I don't deny it. I have no regrets. When I killed him, I was trembling, but then I was completely relaxed. I also killed my friend Qasim who had sex with all the girls I liked in tenth grade. I was shy, couldn't even talk to them. I asked him to take me in his father's fancy car to the highest point on Mount Qasioun. He was drinking as he told me about his time with them, about his sexual prowess despite his inability to satisfy them. He got drunk and bragged about their pictures on his expensive cell phone—a phone we, the poor, would never dream of owning. Then he went out on the cliff overlooking the city and laughed, wicked and loud. I stifled his laughter and pushed him. He rolled down the mountain and died. I came down the mountain running.

A year later Mr. Hani, the history teacher, caught me cursing him from under the seat to cause trouble. He dragged me by my neck to the first row. I grabbed him by his neck in order to keep my crown as 'king of the trouble-makers', a crown I had fashioned for myself. I didn't want to hit him, but when he cursed my mother, all I could see was blood. I smashed his face with my hands. I pushed him to the floor and kicked his head. I lifted him up and banged his head against the metal grid in the third-floor hallway. His face fell back, soaked in blood and imprinted with the grid's squares.

A month after, I was surprised to find out he didn't die. I went to apologize to him so he would drop the charges and save me from prison. I killed him later on.

I stuck a rifle in the behind of the security-force member who arrested me, hit me and spat on me in the detention car. Like a true rascal, I asked: 'Oh, you don't want freedom, huh? What's this for? This is for saying, "Fuck freedom!" '

The head of the publishing house, convinced by his lover, declined to publish my poetry collection despite the committee's approval. I waited for them at night and observed them entering the office where they usually met. I waited a little after the lights were off. I went in and shot them with a pistol affixed with a silencer. I left them there, scandalously naked and dead.

One of the crazy women who calls herself a poet regurgitates naive words at us, words that have nothing to do with creative writing unless you were to call security reports creative. I tried not to hurt her feelings. I spoke to her individually about the linguistic and spelling mistakes, the broken meter, plagiarism and how her text was too on the nose. She was furious, as if someone had peed on her wedding dress. She instigated campaigns against me and accused me of being an enemy of success. A sexist not wanting a woman to be famous! I made this crazy woman breathe under the same water whose metaphor she stole. I placed her in a library of silly books and burnt her along with them!

After every killing operation I undertook, I felt a deep pain in my jaw. I discovered that when I kill, I grind my teeth, my molars in particular. I open my eyes wide so no moment passes without my seeing it. I observe their features. The last look on a human's face before they part from this world. The last sound they utter. The last breath. The last living cell in their body before it goes limp. I admit my cowardice and fear. I avoid quarrelling in front of people. That is why I kill them while we're alone. If someone sees me, I kill them too. To me, heroism is an absolute individual victory. It starts and ends with fear. Fear creates heroism. The one who is never afraid is not a hero. He is nothing but a beast, and beasts do not usually enjoy being monsters!

I killed them all. My younger brother, more spoilt than I. My dad's wife when she cursed my little brother. My mom's husband when he hit her. My mom when she left us as children. My cousin the informant. My uncle the intellectual. Our annoying neighbour. The children who play in the neighbourhood. The Shabbiha militiamen who stomped my car. The father of an old friend who used to hit her. My friend who betrayed me with an ex-lover. The neighbourhood barber who messed up my hair. Our young neighbour's son who turned her from a bright young girl into a mother. The bus driver. The coyote who smuggled people from Turkey to Greece. The German cop who said: 'Have a good day!' after making me pay a fine. Many others I don't remember. I killed them with unprecedented violence, eyes closed thinking they were open. Then I opened them and carried on.

All those I killed in my dreams are still alive. They attack my memory like a single army. They laugh, they dance, they look at me, full of *Schadenfreude*. They did not disappear. There is no solution for ending their existence— it seems—except by killing my own memory!

Many followed in my steps. Many killed. All of you have killed in your dreams, though you may not have admitted it yet!

The Gift
That Killed
Us All

What if you were 'Amr? Close your eyes a little more and you will see a twelve-year-old running towards you, carrying a mountain of blame on his shoulders, driving a shadow of pain many times his age. Close your eyes tighter. You don't need to mess your eyes up in the middle of the day. The sky is clear enough to see the chopper hovering over its prey. The sun is bright enough for the martyrs to avoid it as they ascend to the sky. Silence fell the way it did minutes after the massacre. The massacre repeats without stopping. No one revels in the presence of silence except for the killer. He occupied the sky. He poured his death out like rain and felt euphoric!

What if death cleared some space for life? I would become him, a child with the colour of water before it poured blood. He runs lightly before his friends' body parts weigh him down. He likes *halawat al-jibn*, that semolina-and-cheese-dessert, more than he loves his mother. He opens his mouth, which the Homs neighbourhood has

71

been missing ever since the incident. 'Amr lost his voice, memory and what a child of his age is capable of doing. He became an expert at getting lost in silence. His voice resembled those of children who have no identity. He had your features and those of your children before death closed in on you. All this happened before the sky started sending gifts in the shape of barrel bombs, sometime during the second year of the Syrian explosion. He was used to following the planes with his innocent eyes in order to find a safe spot to play. He didn't have any white hair then. The white hair came later on.

I'm 'Amr. You don't have to believe it. I can't believe it myself. How can the one born into twelve years of sadness not have white hair? How can the son of Death's capital hold onto his memory? Memory loss is the only salvation for going back to the day my mother gave birth to me, a pilgrimage to repent for the pain, to purify all the corpses stuck in my memory that paint the walls of my dreams in red and black. I lost my voice not because I was unable to speak but because I decided to be struck with the disease of wisdom. I am 'Amr, who walked out of his death with no voice, who left his muteness without an alphabet. He left his alphabet because he wanted to instinctively play, but never did. I am 'Amr waiting for an unknown gift from someone he did not know. This gift only comes in dreams, wearing pink and with a blue ribbon. The gift was real on that day except that the children, my friends, ran ahead of me to it. They opened it, and it blew them up. Their body parts fell on me like pieces of candy at weddings. I gathered up their fingers and chunks of flesh as if they were my own. I looked for their features in search of mine. The children's bodies disappeared and turned into scattered pieces that meant nothing on their own! What is the value of these parts if they aren't put back together? I ran all over the place at once, urging an amputated hand to move, a leg that used to kick balls to do so again. The blood is deeper than its red and burning. The dust tries as hard as it can to cover up the crime!

The explosion didn't last long. It took his voice and three souls. It took off without a single complete body. It took my voice and my memory. I am not narrating what I remember but what they told me about it afterwards.

What kind of murderer makes a child's gift into a bomb? Did he look carefully at what his own children love and wrapped the gift in their favorite colours? Did he imagine the scene as he was looking into his children's eyes? What if someone were to do the same thing to them? 'Amr was saved, other than his friends and memories. He made it to one of the refugee camps and the first thing he did was play. He lost his memory but didn't forget how to play football. It took a while for him to regain his ability to speak. Eventually he did. As for his white hair, it didn't turn black again. It remained a witness to the massacre. 'Amr is growing, after being born big with a memory too small for death!

Leave Your Home
and Build Another

Going back kills you. The sigh that stands at screaming's door drags you backward, swallows you. Disappointment is all that's left of you for it to spit out. A woman brings you into a black hole called love. Another saves you and teaches you redemption. A third opens up a life full of breath between two deaths. Young murderers wait for your light to appear at darkness' door. The barks of neighbourhood dogs ring out, denying, gossiping, gnashing at your face. And the revolution . . . Who stands with the revolution other than your voice in this din of barking and wailing, clothes cut from stone buried at the highest point you could think of? Contemplate your fear! Fear is the only thing like you!

They stole the features of your death from the face of a monster. They whipped you like they had before. They pulled a song like a rope around your embrace, trapped you in a lap that pronounces your name. They wrote your name on road signs. They drew you as a stranger in bathrooms full of addicts, grew stories in the consciousness of interrupted narratives. Every man with a bad reputation suddenly becomes generous and pure. Here you are cutting down the dark tree in your mind like a garden of absence, filling in your presence with different colours that have one name. The dark colour does not resemble you, and you do not look like it. No one accepts an honest mirror. No one dares to cut lying's breast in order to wean children off it. No one escapes from tomorrow to the past except for you, me and us, those of us who have been touched by the jinn of yesterday!

Yesterday kills you. The present consoles you as it passes over your stern face. The day kills you. Happiness makes you cry as it waves with an unseen hand to mark your absence. Someone from behind, someone from up ahead kills you not knowing why he kills you except that the order came from above! So be the one up there. Be a spider that kills emptiness as it settles. Write your commandments like threads more powerful than memory. Make shrouds out of them for those trapped inside. Go far away. Let your prey come, full of desire, from all directions. Live far away from the rain. Be gentle with it when it comes your way. Take your belly, turn yourself into a bridge for the grass. Go down, go up. Build your web as carefully as a fisherman would his net. Rest close by and wait. String some webbing between you and the trap to wake you when a newcomer arrives. Don't look! You'll know its size by how it shakes. Release it if it's too big. Release it if you do not like the way it smells. Start with the insides if you like, and leave it an empty, mummified body. Leave your home and build another. Leave something in every home to show how horny you were!

A child running from his innocent features kills you to become a hero. But heroism ends up killing him. It kills whatever can grow in a child who is playing to grow up. There is no hero on that land sown with injustice and war. There is no hero there except for death, standing victorious as it awaits your flesh. The spread-out dirt of worms and intermittent wailing fades to silence. Eventually, you fade too. No one says your name anymore. A child sinking in the drowning sea of death kills you. A child born to be killed kills you! A child born to kill kills you. Yearning, love, family, light, age, God, homeland, and sea kill you. Earth, paradise, memories of old photos, morning's entourage, happiness' waist and exile kill you. Revolution, women of death and grandmother's stories kill you.

Return kills you . . . going back kills you . . .

So, kill them back!

The Minutes Erased
from Yarmouk's
Black Day

They left the way they had over sixty years ago. Nothing is different this time. What they left behind was the same as the first time. What they brought with them was the same as the first time. Nothing is different. They only left what they could not carry. They left houses heavy with memories. They left streets that ate pieces of their feet. They left clothes that carry their smell and guard it under ashes. They left the names themselves: Haifa, Jerusalem, Carmel, Al-Qastal, Al-Tira, Lubya, Safad. They left the old martyrs' cemetery, and the new one too. No one remembered to mention that one of them left behind an automatic laundry machine stuffed with money he had saved for his son's wedding. No one remembered to mention that someone left their music instrument under a table. No one remembered to mention that a teenager left without the pictures of his lovers and notebooks of silly poetry. No one remembered to mention that the new plasma TV was still in its box, its owners unable to try it and gather around the way they do with fire on cold nights. Everyone forgot to say that the children left without their toys, that their breastfeeding mothers left with milk curdling in their breasts. They left the way they did the first time . . . without any features.

Nothing is different. They have the same names, the same destroyed dreams. The murderer is the same even if they changed their name. The corpses are still the same. They left the corpses behind and took off. They were unable to take them along in their second exodus!

One of them asks another: 'Is this the second refuge?'

'No, yesterday taught us not to cling to the tent, except that the camp was not a tent. I will stay. I will go somewhere close by for a few days before returning. I will not become a refugee for a second time.'

'Then stay! I renounce these homelands. I will go far away for my children. If you want, you can cling . . . to death!'

'People who have experienced being a refugee know all too well that they do not want to become another refugee to some unknown land, language and people. There is not enough time for us to start over. Go on and leave . . . I will cling to this death until I live . . . I know this death. A death you know is better than one you don't!'

They left the way they left Palestine. They left what they left, carrying the memories of their destroyed houses. They carried scars matching the number of people in the camp, enough clothes for a couple of days, some of their official papers and the keys to their houses—except this time the keys were smaller in size. The cemetery more crowded with dead bodies than marble. No one knew that the wedding savings the father left behind in the washing machine were sold in bulk at the checkpoint. The soldiers fussed and fought over the musical instrument until it broke over their heads. Should we expect anything different from the military? They left not knowing what happened. Maybe they should not know, so that their feelings about return will stay the same!

A year after they left the camp, they heard that Hassan was tortured to death and was now a martyr. This Hassan, or rather 'that Hassan' did not want to leave the camp. He only wanted to compose one theatrical piece a year and have it performed in the camp. Only in the camp. He did not want to be famous. He wanted to be ordinary, like any other face in the camp. The killer realized how dangerous Hassan was, so he killed him!

We love you so, you dump, you pile of destruction that lies over its lovers' heads. What more would you like than the beautification of your ugliness? What more would you like than our bragging about belonging to you!? We are the children of the destroyed and of destruction, destroyers, destroyed, hungry . . . murderers in the making, projects for the killed and projects for survival. We have no names except tin roofs and the stereotypical image of the 'camp-dweller'. You refugee: displaced, uprooted, persecuted, exiled, martyred! Why did you give the same name to two graveyards!?

They killed Hassan the comedian because they are afraid of a smile. They killed him in the dark. They sent out the hand of darkness to kill us all. Here they are, the murderers of the night, killing in broad daylight in the name of God, in memory of Hassan and people uprooted from the camp. Hassan used to say, 'I like to define myself as a Palestinian Syrian.' He is the son of two deaths, then. His Syrianness killed him just as his Palestinianness did. Whoever is not killed by both is killed by one and stays alive in the other, a dead soul wandering without a tomb. The last thing we heard Hassan say was, 'I remember what Damascus was like in the past . . . I feel as if I won't see her again.' He was right.

They left the way they did the first time. Nothing was different. They were pronounced the way Hassan's body pronounced his soul. This is what the Syrian MiG jets did to them. This is what the Syrian Security Branch's Palestine Division did to Hassan. This is what the extremists did to those who remained under siege.

Who Threw the Key
in the River?

As you cross the Rhine river, you come across some colourful locks. You pass them, eagerly descending, curious. You start to count your breaths as they come faster. A bridge, a piece of metal hanging in the air, comes between you and falling. Falling was the fate of the sad, drowning keys. You spend a lot of time contemplating the story and hoping to become a lock— not a key. Being metal left to rust is better than drowning!

Crucified bodies are locks that cannot tell their stories. Thousands of love stories hang naked, except for their mystery. They look with burning desire towards the river in search of the drowned keys. A bridge for love stretches from a bank that lies before sighing to the one after it. You might think the story is only about the ones who have the lock and the key, but it is nothing like that.

The key is a self, drowning in secrets and the fingerprints of its owners. Nobody but the keys and their owners know if the fingerprints are the same on other keys. The bubbles under the bridge are not from fish. There are no fish between the ships and their engines. The bubbles are the scandals of lovers that the keys tell and leave behind like foam.

The mute locks are not disturbed by the caress of passers-by or the sounds of the express trains that make the bridge tremble. They do not care about the keys' crying for help in their attempt to come together to build a floating tower for revenge. The locks carry the names of their owners. It's not necessarily a bad thing to have the same name on more than one lock. There's no need either to talk about a feminist movement started by the locks against the patriarchy of the keys. Each could be male or female, or neither. It's important to write about the one's longing for the other. The first, the lock, wants the other, even if they don't want to be opened and released. The other, the key, wants the first, even if they do not want to save them from sinking. What happens when they part ways? Would they dare release the chain of the lock and throw it to its mate?

There are different names and nationalities, some going back more than forty years. There are some Arabic names, even if only a few. We do not know what happened to their owners. We do not know their religion, sect, colour, whether they are alive or dead, separated like the lock and the key or still together. Did they survive the war? We do not even know their position on the Arab Spring! I know that many of these stories were sad or had sad endings. They were not always as beautiful as the colours of the locks on the bridge. These sad, ugly stories have to be there. Without them, the beautiful, uplifting ones would have no taste. They build the myth of their beauty on the ugliness of others.

One day, the story of this bridge will also end. The love stories grew heavy and the bridge is on the verge of collapse. Don't leave your stories there. Love weighs heavily on steel. Beautiful colours are about to destroy this shrine. Bridges can be rebuilt if they fall down, but who will rebuild a hundred thousand stories and names? Who will save the drowning stories and document the meeting between the locks and their keys?

The Seller of Love
and Their Bed

I am the seller of love. I carry an empty bottle of water, a piece of soap and a used handkerchief. I wait for it to rain. I light a candle and blow on it the way I used to blow on hot food. I make a hearty meal out of the candle's fragrance. Here I stand before you, covered in an absurdity you call filth. I haven't combed my hair since the last time I bought a brush, even though I sit in front of the mirror for hours. I do not see myself!

I am the seller of love. Who told you about my religion but didn't mention my name? How could they know my religion if they don't know me? I am who I am. I have a thin body with tender bones and skin made of glass. I have eyes, regular other than their fear, moles whose number matches that of my old lovers. I have wrinkles starting to show that something is breaking down there in the distance, between the ribs of my exhausted chest!

I used to be faster, smooth-faced, with bright eyes. I had a sly look that mastered the art of hunting for love.

I feel impotent now. I sit open-mouthed, with unfocused eyes, absent-minded in an expanse of emptiness that stretches to nowhere. A young woman who does not speak my language sits before me. I no longer know the language of her eyes. She looks at me. I pay attention. She runs away with her eyes. People pay attention to me staring at her as if I wanted to harass her! She smiles without moving her lips after seeing how red my cheeks had gotten—the small part where my beard doesn't grow yet. She keeps looking even though I've forgotten how to make a move. I put on a coat that's not my size, and take off. Who was it that called a coat a *mi'taf* in Arabic, a word that shares its root with emotion?

I am the lonely seller of love. I'm stuck in bed, living in it as if it were my mother's womb. Seven huge cups of coffee, empty. I recently put the coffee machine next to the bed. The last drops of a Coke bottle gone flat, the wrappers of some anti-depressant chocolates, an overflowing ashtray and paper napkins all over the place, each one with its own story. The seller of love is becoming a customer of imagination and admirer of paper napkins. Zits started popping up on my face as if I were a teenager—the beard was another strategic choice! There's a strange relation between me and the bed. It is the only one capable of enduring my weird behaviour. I sold lots of love in the past, but I won't sell my bed now. Who could sell themselves?

A multipurpose bed, square. It substituted for a writing table for a long time and witnessed romantic battles between me and my imagination. It drinks coffee with me in the morning and eats the meals I conjure up. The bed's addicted to smoking. It knows many names that have never got near it. It recognizes sounds that ears have never heard! It knows the secrets I keep, loads of scandals and beautiful, strange stories. It hates the light like me. Who could sell this loyal treasure?

I am the seller of love, and I'll die one day. When I do, don't tell my bed new secrets. Who was it that made these words so similar? *Sirr*—a 'secret'; *sarir*—a 'bed'; *asrar*—'secrets'; *asirra*—'beds'. Don't give the bed more than it can handle. Carry out what Jep Gambardella said to a woman he was teaching: 'You need to respect the rituals of the funeral. Go to the person who was closest to the deceased, hold their hands in yours and briefly say:

'"In the coming days, whenever you feel lonely, you can always rely on me!"

'Don't cry more than his relatives. Don't take the lights of sadness away from them—it's forbidden to do so!'

Do no more than that. Just carry out their wish, and if you want to do more good, make measurements for a coffin, or burn the two of us and spread our ashes together! This is how the tired seller of love and his bed can finally rest!

*Ever Since
I Did Not
Die*

Ever since I did not die, I've become a mouse and I chomp on borrowed time. I make a space out of every corner and peel off the covers of books before I am stuck in the trap of fear. I get lost among the pillars of monumental churches looking for a familiar face not swallowed by forgetting. I pull a girl to my manhood and exhaust her with life. I look at death with the eyes of lust. I carry migrations whose pain my passport endured for an insanity that does not end. My autobiography is their names, their voices, the features of those who survived yesterday and every second that recognized me after we bumped into each other.

I was born when I did not die! Four stones that lost their way to falling. They missed my head which had gotten rid of all that came before. One stone fell, broken with a childhood I never noticed. Another hung the women of before-death from their breasts and crashed down. Another broke through superstitions about God, his masculinity and the stories of a Palestinian grandmother running away from a defeat she rejects and fights against with delusions. The last one fell, and I noticed a broken smile saying, 'You are my lipstick.'

Five years. The sixth is a child I could not bear. I threw him in the garbage. I don't know in what land he was burnt, buried or recycled in the shape of a clock reminding me I did not die. The first is in a land I did not choose. The second is in a prison that opened a door to the sun through a sewage pipe. The third is in a lap that taught me not to give up. The fourth is in the lap that lost my warmth. The fifth is in the window of realization about how I survived, how I drove death into exile and threw it away. I shove poetry, melted in the fire of love, into its ears to wipe its memory. Then I bite its ears so it will never return!

Ever since I did not die, I started to taste beauty. I open war's door, the chapter of fear, and sink further into the hatred of heroism. I shed all I thought was right for love. There is no reality in believing. Believing is the enemy of reality. Identity is everything except for place, flag, race, religion and gender. Ever since I did not die, I have lost my identity. I do not care much if I carry one or it carries me! Longing for something you never chose is one of the absurdities a dictatorship leaves behind—I know that 'dictatorship' is too direct but I opened the dictionaries of all the languages in the world and couldn't find a poetic equivalent! With time, the country began to act like a tyrant. It perpetuated our disfiguration from the inside. We started to beautify the ugliness we had got used to until it became our measure for beauty! Is there anything worse than longing for what can't be longed for? Covering up whatever the cosmetic industry can't make beautiful!? I hate these totalitarian, patriarchal countries!

Ever since I did not die and even before, she was the sincerest person I knew, the warmest person I ever came across despite becoming a piercing piece of ice when she found out about my involvement with other women. I know her well. I know how her fruits matured before their time. I know how she aged in my lap for two years while reading my features like a creator who regrets the unintended placement of a mole that multiplied until it became an entire army of birth defects. I know how the war hurt her womb, how loss closed its door on her. With all my disappointment and fear, I grew distant, not wanting death to gloat as it approached.

'The son of the tent refuses to have a homeland.'

I say it, then I hesitate: how can I confirm the image of a homeland I refuse? What keeps a homeland from moving around? It gets old, sags, cries, gets angry, leaves, stabs, escapes, drowns in the sea, survives. It retells the story of those who didn't die. It creates a fake identity card, comes to you for a hug, then leaves! How stupid is a person who searches when they've gone astray, when they break all the furniture in the house looking for the glasses they're already wearing!

Even when we have a homeland, we travel, afraid, cold, in love, and searching. We travel because travel is part of our instinct for life. 'Birds that don't migrate don't deserve wings!'

I say what has been said before and fly off like a flock of pigeons kept by someone whose testimony is inadmissible. I see the camp from above. It looks like my closet. She always said that my closet looked like a bomb had gone off in it. I remember this as I land like a flock of madness on her belly button. She sinks down. I fly off but don't go high. I hold fast to her chest and breath, knowing that she is the only one who exhales pure oxygen. I peck at her skin, one grain of wheat at a time. I get drunk on love as if I did not die, as if I did not kill my children and throw them in the water, in the desert, on the bodies of imagination, and in the wombs of necessity, as if I were a minaret singing songs of love for a simple God who does not swing a stick or bless the water. I write about death, not life. You don't write about life, you live it!

I go back and remember how we exchanged a quick hello in Damascus, how the voice of freedom was louder than our ability to exchange names. We met again to announce a hunger strike in front of worrying workers in Amman. We met for a third time, got separated for two hours, then met again by chance and never separated again!

There's a mistake in the calculation of gravity, wind speeds and weight of stones. There's another mistake in the sniper's lens, a third in the targeting of a bomb, a fourth in a city where a poet is not appropriately welcomed, a fifth in the walls of a prison the size of my head I'm trying to escape, a sixth in an unintended resemblance to my friend that allowed me to use his passport, a seventh, eighth, ninth and tenth. They led me to her bed along with the other mistakes that brought us together. Our love is a product of mistakes that, had I died, would have never happened! My love is the son of fear, the son of the many names I've carried: Marcel, Yazan, Salah, Abdul-Rahman, Jihad. I don't remember if there were others. I admit to my fear, the most honest feeling I've known and a sincere friend who has accompanied me for a long time without quarrel or estrangement. That is why I did not die. If I had, I would have become a hero, but I don't find anything deserving in heroism.

Afterword

LEVI THOMPSON

Ramy Al-Asheq is a poet, through and through, so what are we to make of this collection of prose pieces? They challenge us to redefine our conception of poetry versus prose as they, like their author, cross borders. Al-Asheq suggests that we might call what you have in your hands 'just a collection of texts, texts that could bear a name' but he—like the texts themselves—resists this incessant need to classify things according to their form. Yes, we have here a book, but that is only because these texts have been bound together as such. Al-Asheq also suggests that what we have before us is a testimony. These texts bear witness to the ineffable experiences of war, escape and migration, collected in a language that frequently crosses the boundaries between prose and poetry much in the same way their author has crossed the boundaries between countries (from Syria, to Jordan, to Germany) and states of being.

Like these texts, Al-Asheq's identity resists categorization. He is a Palestinian raised in the Yarmouk Refugee Camp in Damascus, Syria; a Syro-Palestinian dissident jailed during the political upheavals that followed the Arab Spring in Syria; a stateless escapee living under an assumed identity in Amman, Jordan; and now, finally, an Arab poet and journalist living in exile in Germany. He occupies several identities at once or, alternatively, none at all, as the title essay, the final one in this collection, might indicate. 'I was born when I did not die,' he tells us. Born into what? In these pieces, Al-Asheq explores various identities into which one might be born beyond the accidents of place and time. We find, instead, a whole range of possibilities in the world of language. 'Identity is everything,' Al-Asheq tells us, 'except for place, flag, race, religion and gender'. In making an escape from totalitarian, patriarchal dictatorship (not only of the Assad regime), he thereby opens up something new, something that lies beyond the usual rules of identity.

'Ever since I did not die, I have lost my identity,' he continues. We have here the central proposition of these texts, one which works in two directions. The first implication is that in death—perhaps only in death—one finds their identity; identity becomes fixed to a person after they have died in how they are either remembered or forgotten. The second must then be that identity becomes more fluid once one has faced down death and lived to tell the tale. These texts, then, are the stories of someone who has conquered death and returned, transformed by the experience and ready to face death again a thousand times over. Al-Asheq has come back from the brink to tell us the stories of the imprisoned, the exiled and the dead.

Although these texts are presented in prose, their author's language disregards the borders between poetic and prosaic, sacred and profane, living and dead. In the first essay of the collection, we find the 'dead-alive'—a character I first came across in Iraqi poet Abd al-Wahhab al-Bayati's existential poetry from the 1960s, a poetry defined by mythic cycles of death and rebirth—'walk[ing] across the crooked path towards a lesser death'. The Arabic of this 'crooked path' contrasts sharply with the 'straight path' or the *sirat mustaqim* that all Muslims are called to follow, and to which Muslims ask God to guide them in the first chapter of the Qur'an, the 'Fatiha', the Opening. The word *sirat* also calls to mind the treacherous bridge a hair's breadth wide that believers must navigate on the Day of Judgment. Al-Asheq plays with these notions, mixing the religious with the secular in order to challenge any strict delineations between the two. In his reimagining of the Resurrection, soldiers stand at the bridge, asking those who cross about their religion, their God and their Book. The Prophet Muhammad, whom some of the faithful believe will be there to intercede and help them across, is nowhere to be found. Al-Asheq transforms the sacred into the profane and the profane into the sacred. His dead-alive cross the crooked path 'only to be thrown once again into the hell that is the tent for seventy more years'. By centering the experiences of the refugees from the camp, he calls out for a transformation of this world, for justice to be carried out for them on earth instead of only after their deaths, that is, for the dead-alive to be given a chance to actually live.

This call issues from several speakers throughout the collection, each of them marginalized or forgotten in some way. We hear the voices of refugees, victims of war, the dead, the jailed, and those buried in the past, in memory. By blurring the boundaries between poetry and prose in their language, the essays formally enact the boundary crossing they call for in their content. Therefore, this collection is more than the sum of its parts, which Al-Asheq has 'gathered [. . .] like someone collecting body parts. Here are the pieces of my body,' he tells us, 'haphazardly brought together in a paper bag.' Although he asks us to 'save this collection from classification', we might consider its parts altogether as a testament to how one individual's experiences crisscross with those of a disparate collective to give that person a new identity and to give a voice, however fractured, to the collective once again.

Notes

Page 5

'A few days before (*Al-Ba'th*)': The Arab Socialist Ba'th Party has ruled in Syria since 1963. The noun *ba'th* means 'resurrection' in Arabic.

Page 9

'I cannot exist . . . unless there is a refugee': From Ammar Ahmad Al-Shuqairy, 'Crisis of Roots' in *The Storytellers as Themselves* (Jordan: Dar Fadaat, 2012).

Page 10

' . . . consider it a privilege': Palestinian writer Saleem al-Beik said in an interview ('The Palestinian Intellectual and the Syrian Revolution: Disappointment or Erasure', *Al-Ayyaam*, 2015) that 'Palestinians have monopolized tragedies, believing their case to be about privilege.'

' . . . live in tents': This is in reference to Yarmouk Refugee Camp in the Syrian capital Damascus where a university classmate posed this question to us in 2009.

' . . . and darkness was upon the face of the deep': Genesis 1:2.

Page 11

' . . . adding features in bright oil on their foreheads': Palestinian Syrian refugees used to say that they had similar foreheads because of the oil they used to get from international aid organizations.

Page 12

'. . . accused of infiltrating paradise': Palestinians coming from Syria have been detained in Camp Cyber City on the Syrian-Jordanian border from May 2012 until today (May 2016). According to their own accounts, they were held under house arrest with a media blackout following a royal political security decree.

'They are tossed into the hell of war seventy times': Tossing is a term the Jordanian authorities used for Syrian and Palestinian refugees who were ordered to return to Syria. They used to toss the refugees at the border to fend for themselves.

Page 13

'The long-time refugees are now called "without"': Stateless means without a homeland, or *staatenlos* in German. European Union countries categorized Palestinians from Syria as stateless. This is written on their official documents.

Page 19

'They have the same letters, but the form is different!' The same letters (*b*, *h* and *r*) are used for sea and war in Arabic but in a different order: حرب وبحر

Page 97

'rituals of the funeral': A reference to Paolo Sorrentino's 2013 film, *The Great Beauty*.

Page 104

'worrying workers in Amman': This is in reference to the United Nations workers who always 'express concern' about what is happening in Syria.